The Consolations of the Cross

ADDRESSES ON THE SEVEN WORDS
OF THE DYING LORD

GIVEN AT S. STEPHEN'S CHURCH
BOSTON, ON GOOD FRIDAY, 1902
TOGETHER WITH TWO SERMONS

BY

Rt. Rev. C. H. Brent, D.D.

WIPF & STOCK · Eugene, Oregon

Wipf and Stock Publishers
199 W 8th Ave, Suite 3
Eugene, OR 97401

The Consolations of the Cross
Addresses on the Seven Words of the Dying Lord
By Brent, C. H.
Softcover ISBN-13: 978-1-6667-6106-1
Hardcover ISBN-13: 978-1-6667-6107-8
eBook ISBN-13: 978-1-6667-6108-5
Publication date 10/4/2022
Previously published by Longmans, Green, and Co., 1919

This edition is a scanned facsimile of the original edition
published in 1919.

TO

HENRY MARTYN TORBERT

MY BELOVED BROTHER IN THE MINISTRY

AND FELLOW WORKER IN THE LORD

WHO NOW RESTS IN PARADISE

．．

I shall not wholly die. Some part,
Nor that a little, shall
Escape the dark destroyer's dart,
And his grim festival.

Contents

IF any excuse will avail for adding to the many books of addresses on the Seven Last Words, I would urge that these contained in this little volume were my last utterance on the Passion to the congregation whom I served through nearly my entire ministry. Originally I had no intention of writing them out, and I have at length done so at the repeated request of some of those who heard them. Though notes taken at the time were put in my hands, I have not tried to reproduce my exact language, which has gone beyond recall.

A tropical sun and the breezes of many seas have been my companions as I have prepared these pages, which I now conclude in my new home on the first anniversary of the day on which the addresses were delivered. They carry with them a loving, yearning look toward happy days among a loyal and forbearing people, upon whom may God's blessing forever rest.

The motive which prompts the publication in this volume of the two sermons forming the appendix is obvious. They are connected intimately with the severing of ties which God bound a while since, and which in His own way and time God broke.

Bishop's House, Manila, P. I.
    Good Friday, 1903.

The Consolations of the Cross

. .

Prelude

*Blessed be the God and Father of our Lord Jesus Christ,
the Father of mercies and God of all comfort; who com-
forteth us in all our affliction, that we may be able to
comfort them that are in any affliction, through the comfort wherewith we ourselves are comforted of God. For
as the sufferings of Christ abound unto us, even so our
comfort also aboundeth through Christ.* 2 COR. i, 3–5.

THE Cross of Christ has an unfailing
attraction for us in that it touches every
human life, and ministers to every human
need. It is a present power, not an echo from
the past; it is not an idea let loose to take
care of itself and find lodgement where it will,
but a force controlled by the hand of Him
who transformed it from a means of torture
and death into the way of consolation and
life. To-day we are not going to spend our
time merely in the consideration of an historic happening and an historic Person. We
shall look back of course, but we shall reach
up for present help, for the Cross is a present
power and the historical Christ is the present Christ,—Jesus "the same yesterday, to

day, and for ever." He has ever before Him
and in Him those human experiences that
culminated in the Cross. His sympathy is
instant, and He is ever ready to pour the
abundance of His strength into our lives.
We read the inspired story that tells us what
He *was*, that we may know what He *is*; we
learn what He *thought*, that we may know
what He *thinks*; the record of what He *did*
is valuable because it reveals to us what He
does. As He lived — that is essentially, in-
wardly — He lives; as He loved, He loves,
—"the same yesterday, to day, and for
ever." He did not fling away His humanity
after His mortal career on earth had closed,
but retained it as a sacred thing, as the shrine
of His experiences among men, as the link
to bind men to Him. Imbedded in His personality, each incident shining as a jewel in
His memory as an ever present fact, is the
history of His life, passion, and death. The
man Christ Jesus upon whom we look back
in the tragic story of the crucifixion is He
to whom we look up. It is all one — what
He was and what He is: to see Him as He
was yesterday is to see Him as He is to-day:

Prelude

the God of strength, the God of love.

We are going to consider Christ in His sufferings rather than the sufferings of Christ. The contemplation of Christ's sufferings can easily become a trap for emotional and morbid natures to shut men out from Him. Too often the preacher has made the Passion the centre of interest and the Person of Christ the incident, whereas Christ is all in all, and the Passion a background throwing Him into relief. His personality is that which must enchain our attention as we try to relate ourselves afresh to Him, so that we shall receive new strength and hope to take up again our lives and our work.

He is indeed the Strong One. His is the only human life of which is recorded no failure; there is not a shadow of fault in His character or a line of defeat in His history. So we turn to Him for strength, for life. But in this day of strenuous living we are apt to lose sight of the tender side of His character. He is God the Consoler as well as God the Strengthener. To remember the former only is to become sentimental; to think of the latter alone is to become hard and sto-

Prelude

ical. Human life has the double need, — the
need of strength and the need of consolation. These having been given, there should
emerge that glorious combination of strength
and tenderness which forms the most win-
some as well as the most powerful of charac-
ters. And so what Christ is, man according
to his measure becomes — strengthener, consoler; such is his wonderful destiny. We ask
Christ for strength, that we may give what
we get to the weak; for consolation, that we
may extend sympathy to the distressed.

He is the Consoler, and never was He
more so than when He was the Sufferer on
the Cross. We all aim to pass through life
with a smile on our lips. It is a recognized
duty that most of the time at any rate we
should wear our sorrows in the deeps and
not on the surface of our lives. It is a nice
courtesy, more than that a delicate considerateness due our fellows, that every man
should bear his own burden. But even when
the face is adorned with gladness, our inner
world aches with the hidden pains and sorrows. Ofttimes behind a hard-won serenity
of countenance resides such tragedy, such

[4]

suffering, as lies beyond the reach of merely human aid: indeed what man or woman who is trying to live seriously has not an infinite need which can be met by nothing short of infinite wisdom and sympathy? We must turn to Christ as the Consoler if we are to continue human, if we are to be saved from bitterness and despair with advancing age, if we are to grow in gentleness and thoughtfulness in our relationship with mankind. O Lord, to Thy gift of strength add that of consolation.

Christ the Sufferer is in a special sense *Christus Consolator*, and to-day we approach Him as such. His seven last utterances are seven points of light, each with a radiance and a colour of its own, each a source of consolation in which to find the very balm that will suit our special need. He who spoke long years ago will speak again as we commemorate the crucifixion, will speak in the old terms but with a new application. He will not fail us. He is the Prince of Peace, and gives to those who seek, that otherwise unattainable peace, without which human nature withers and dies.

[5]

I

The Consolation of Christ's Intercession

Father, forgive them; for they know not what they do. S. LUKE xxiii, 34.

OUR memory is filled with the story of the Passion as given by the four Evangelists, and it will not be necessary to repeat it. We shall only refer briefly to the events without endeavouring to supplement or paraphrase them; there is a beauty and directness in the matchless narrative of Holy Writ that cannot be improved upon by rhetoric.

The trial is over, and the journey of pain and of patience has been made. At Calvary Jesus is met by the ill-directed but well-meaning consolation of the cup that stupefies; but He will not quench his thirst at the expense of the full control of His mental faculties. He is stripped and fixed to the Cross. As the soldiers complete their task of crucifixion, He utters a prayer when we would expect a moan, a prayer which has echoed the world through ever since,—"Father, forgive them; for they know not what they do."

What consolation in this word for us! When human life is at its worst, and uncontrolled passions hold complete sway, Jesus sees hope for the poor victims and prays for their redemption. Greater degradation than that which surrounded the Cross the world has never known. He prays for His murderers in particular, but after a life of intercessory prayer one cannot prescribe limits to a petition. We learn to pray for the many by praying for the one; but a day will break when the prayer for one becomes the prayer for many. All who share a common need come flocking into the shelter of our prayer. There is no forbidding them even if we would; nor does it detract from the depth or earnestness of the prayer for one. This is true of every man who has learned through years of watching and years of wrestling how to pray; how much more is it true of Christ! Yes, He prayed for His murderers, and as He prayed for them a whole world of men and women came flowing in a beseeching tide and flooded His petition. The least

Christ's Intercession

transgressor as well as the greatest sought
and found place there.

Men want assurance, daily assurance, that
they are not without hope, that God still
has a future for them, and here it is. His
prayer made clear there was hope for the
worst, and if for the worst, then for all.
Moreover, Christ's prayer was offered not
at a time when He could marvel at man's
faith. He hoped when things were their
blackest. We can applaud and anticipate
final success when our fellows are doing their
best, we can hope for humanity then. But
Christ hoped when His work of salvation
seemed a failure and human life was at its
worst. Even His chosen comrades had denied and abandoned Him. So, I say, this
word consoles us, and shines like a beacon
at moments when new failure, new shame
has driven us out on the barren waste of despair. The knowledge that God still hopes for
us renews hope for ourselves in our hearts.

But we have been looking back: now
let us look up. What do we see yonder at
God's right hand? We see the unchanged,
unchangeable Jesus making intercession for

[9]

us,—not with a mere lip intercession, but with an intercession in which His full, unblemished humanity speaks and pleads. The intercession of our heavenly Advocate is no empty cry, no shallow request. It is as efficacious as it is unceasing, as deep as the love of God, as broad as human life. "He is able to save to the uttermost them that draw nigh unto God through Him, seeing He ever liveth to make intercession for them." He who loved His own on earth to the uttermost and to the end, loves still with the same love. He saves men *to* the uttermost as well as *from* the uttermost. The best is His gift for those who have been the worst and have *drawn near unto God*.

Such is the consolation of the first Word from the Cross,—the consolation of knowing beyond peradventure that God has hope for us, hope for us now when our sins array themselves before our eyes in forbidding ranks, hope for us when human hope lies paralyzed and all but dead; the consolation of the perpetual and availing intercession of Christ that stops at asking nothing less than God's best. The returning prodigal is not

Christ's Intercession

left forgiven, but naked and sick and alone;
as the next word shows, he is saved to the
uttermost. Sandals are on his feet, the best
robe on his shoulders, and he has the com-
radeship of a Father who presses kisses on
his brow.

As we receive so must we give. We must
learn to hope with a steadier, larger hope
for others. Let us cease caging men in an
evil heredity when the heredity of sonship
in God is their portion; let us cease believing the latest novel of the decadence that
pictures society as hopelessly rotten, making a decayed apple-tree the symbol of an
orchard. Men will become what we hope.
Hope is not a courtesy, it is a vitalizing
energy; and it blossoms into prayer, rich
full prayer for others. We must unite our intercessions with Christ's. Shall we not spend
in these three hours part of our devotions
on others? We will look for the consolation
of His intercessions; then being consoled,
we will console. Putting self aside we will
wrap a robe of hope around those about us
—the worst as well as the best.

Let us pray for those who are near to us

and touch our lives, and we will find that others will also creep under the shadow of our prayer. We will pray for great things for them, a leaping prayer to Him who saves from and to the uttermost. Let us pray for the ignorant and the sinning; those who have wronged us, or those who we think have wronged us; and those whom we have wronged.

JESU, Lord of life and glory,
  Bend from heaven Thy gracious ear;
While our waiting souls adore Thee,
    Friend of helpless sinners, hear:
      By Thy mercy,
      Oh, deliver us, good Lord.

From the depths of nature's blindness,
    From the hardening power of sin,
From all malice and unkindness,
    From the pride that lurks within,
      By Thy mercy,
      Oh, deliver us, good Lord.

When temptation sorely presses,
    In the day of Satan's power,
In our times of deep distresses,
    In each dark and trying hour,
      By Thy mercy,
      Oh, deliver us, good Lord.

Christ's Intercession

When the world around is smiling,
  In the time of wealth and ease,
Earthly joys our hearts beguiling,
  In the day of health and peace,
    By Thy mercy,
  Oh, deliver us, good Lord.

In the weary hours of sickness,
  In the times of grief and pain,
When we feel our mortal weakness,
  When all human help is vain,
    By Thy mercy,
  Oh, deliver us, good Lord.

In the solemn hour of dying,
  In the awful judgment day,
May our souls, on Thee relying,
  Find Thee still our hope and stay:
    By Thy mercy,
  Oh, deliver us, good Lord.

SILENT PRAYER·

O LORD, *we beseech thee, absolve thy people from their offences; that through thy bountiful goodness we may all be delivered from the bands of those sins, which by our frailty we have committed. Grant this, O heavenly Father, for Jesus Christ's sake, our blessed Lord and Saviour.*

II

The Consolation of Present Peace and Anticipated Joy

Verily I say unto thee, To-day shalt thou be with Me in Paradise. S. LUKE xxiii, 43.

WE often reverently wonder what meant the silences of the Cross. We dwell a great deal, and rightly enough, on Christ's words, but what of the hours of unbroken quiet? Of what was He thinking? Out of the fulness of the heart the mouth speaketh; what Christ thought He said. The words are the key to the silences.

The second Word tells us that during the time that had elapsed since He first spoke, His mind was on the life of the world to come, that new country as yet unexplored even by Him, upon the painful threshold of which He was now trembling. The prayer of the dying robber breaks in on His thoughts, thoughts which fit the prayer. With assurance and swift readiness He responds by promising the rest and joy of which He was thinking to His companion in suffering.

A considerable time seems to have elapsed

since the first Word, enough for the wonderful converting power of Christ to work upon the soul of the robber who ultimately became penitent under its influence. This robber, stung by his pain, half intoxicated from the drugged cup, was in no condition to be moved by spiritual influences at the beginning. Probably he helped his fellow to taunt Jesus at first. Soon, however, the momentary effect of the liquor passed away, and with senses rendered acute by suffering he saw quickly and deeply. Unlike his companion, he threw open his soul to the subtle power breathed forth from the central Figure. Touched by His patience, recalling perhaps the loving prayer that fell on half deaf ears when it was uttered, repentance was more rapidly perfected than with most men. The conditions of the Cross made this possible. With the majority of us repentance is a slow and laborious process; here it is as swift as it is royal. His recorded words contain all the elements of that sorrow of soul which is the preface to peace and joy. He separates himself from his former companion in sin and rebukes him with quiet, selfless dignity. He vindicates the righteousness of Christ and bows his spirit in simple faith at the feet of the King. His sense of unworthiness allows him to ask but little even of a king—only that he may not be forgotten. Christ rewards his penitence by blessing him with a benediction so full that it blesses all ages with its consoling touch. "Verily I say unto thee, To-day shalt thou be with Me in Paradise."

Hereafter the penitent robber sinks into patient silence and meditates on the wealth of the promise.

Our Lord's answer tells us three things: (1) the blessing of forgiveness; (2) the reality of the world to come; (3) the character of that world.

1. Forgiveness is a great and wonderful word containing in its small compass the whole story of redemption. And those two words "with Me" are its sufficient explanation. A theology which is fast passing into oblivion once stripped it of its royal robes. It was a forensic process, a condescension of Divine pity, cold and exact, remitting some penalty. Christ declares it to be a renewal of abundant life by a renewal of the privilege of

[17]

close fellowship and union with Him. When
God forgives man He bestows upon him the
highest honour in His gift. The courtier in
the outer chambers of the palace feels privi-
leged; but the heavenly King bids each penitent subject come and share his compan-
ionship—"with Me in Paradise." In the
first Word our Lord prays for forgiveness
for men; in the second He reveals the character of that for which He prayed by ministering to the first fruits of his prayer.

Oh, children of men! are you taking the
joy that is offered you, the present joy in all
its completeness of forgiveness? or are you
trying to satisfy your appetite with crumbs
when the whole loaf is yours? Whatever the
past, God can remit more than you can commit. And his remission means admission into his presence.

2. The reality of the world to come! In this
past year bitter partings and unlooked-for
sorrows have entered into our lives. Friends
have gone into new and distant fields of labour; we have been bereaved as individuals,
as a parish, as a nation; and we ought to dwell
much on the reality of the world to come.

Present Peace and Anticipated Joy

It is only when that other world becomes
more real than this that we can face bereavement not simply with fortitude, but with
bounding hope. Christ speaks of Paradise
with firm assurance; and of going thither as
though it might be to Jerusalem or Caper-
naum. He has been thinking much about it,
and when He speaks of it to His new-found
follower His tones carry conviction so that
he too rejoices in anticipation of the beau-
tiful land yonder where he is to be with the
King. The penitent robber thinks crudely
no doubt of that new country. To him it is
a place of physical delight where the wind
blows through stately palms, and glad riv-
ers race to the sea over fertile plains. But it
is real, a land near by. He and his Companion, Christ, are but a step away, for they are
to enter it *to-day*.

Our realization of that land at best must
be crude. But do not let us be afraid of talking
of Paradise and Heaven as *places*. Doubtless
they are *conditions*. But the common mind
does not grasp what is baldly transcendental.
We must be more or less anthropomorphic,
we must project our ideas of life as we know

it beyond the grave. Nor is there any reason to be ashamed of so doing. Christ chose a term, "Paradise," suited to the comprehension of the man He was dealing with. He gave him something concrete, real. The metaphysician might find occasion to cavil at the materialism lurking behind the word. But Christ used it because it had substance for the ex-robber, it was something upon which he could exercise a living faith. Look up then to that real land where in quiet joy dwell your loved ones who have gone before.

3. Its chief characteristic is joyousness. Paradise is a glad word, fragrant with delight. Oh, yes, call it Purgatory if you will, if by Purgatory you mean a place where the last traces of sin are done away by the boundless tenderness of God. But the souls at rest are happy suffering souls; our earliest experience there will be to feel the caress of God. Paradise is not a prison house of torture; it is a palace of joy. The name tells of the Garden of God where He is the sufficient Food, and where the redeemed, transfigured, move from strength to strength in endless progress toward perfection; a garden where there is

Present Peace and Anticipated Joy

fellowship—"with Me"; where "angel faces smile which we have loved long since and lost awhile." A young girl who lay dying had thought so much about the fellowship in Paradise that others caught her radiant belief and sent messages to their friends by her: wife to husband, child to parent, mother to baby. Messages so multiplied that she could not retain all in her memory, but she treasured the messages that came from mothers to their babies. To that dying girl how joyous a place was Paradise which long since became her home.

And God wishes Paradise to begin now inasmuch as He invites us to be with Him now. Soon, sooner than we dream of perhaps, we shall be bidden to move out and up through the gate of death to join the souls at rest. There we shall wait for the final triumph. God speed the day when the joys of Paradise shall rise to the still greater completeness of Heaven! for

. . . . lo! there breaks a yet more glorious day;
The Saints triumphant rise in bright array;
The King of Glory passes on His way.
Alleluia!

𝕮𝖍𝖊 𝕮𝖔𝖓𝖘𝖔𝖑𝖆𝖙𝖎𝖔𝖓 𝖔𝖋

Let us give thanks for the faithful departed,—for relatives, friends, and those of our parish who have entered into rest.

OH, what, if we are Christ's,
    Is earthly shame or loss?
Bright shall the crown of glory be
    When we have borne the cross.

Keen was the trial once,
    Bitter the cup of woe,
When martyred saints, baptized in blood,
    Christ's sufferings shared below.

Bright is their glory now,
    Boundless their joy above,
Where, on the bosom of their God,
    They rest in perfect love.

Lord, may that grace be ours,
    Like them in faith to bear
All that of sorrow, grief, or pain
    May be our portion here:

Enough if Thou at last
    The word of blessing give,
And let us rest beneath Thy feet,
    Where saints and angels live.

SILENT PRAYER

Present Peace and Anticipated Joy

WE bless thy holy Name for all thy servants departed this life in thy faith and fear; beseeching thee to give us grace so to follow their good examples, that with them we may be partakers of thy heavenly kingdom. Grant this, O Father, for Jesus Christ's sake, our only Mediator and Advocate.

GRANT, we beseech thee, merciful Lord, to thy faithful people pardon and peace, that they may be cleansed from all their sins, and serve thee with a quiet mind; through Jesus Christ our Lord.

III

The Consolation of
Christ's Love of Home and Nation

Woman, behold thy Son! . . . Behold thy Mother!
S. JOHN xix, 26, 27.

AS yet no word of sympathy had been uttered *for* Christ: all sympathy had been from Him for others. But at last the two from whom He would most desire an expression of sympathy come nigh,—Mary, the Lord's mother, and John, the beloved disciple; the Virgin and the virgin-souled. John had brought her that she might be near her Son. Perhaps just now the rabble had begun to disperse and the Cross could be reached easily. At any rate they are close enough to catch words spoken from the Cross as they stand in silent sympathy gazing at Him. He sees and recognizes their pain. But He has consolation for them, the consolation of new responsibility: "Woman, behold thy Son! . . . Behold thy Mother! And from that hour that disciple took her to his own home." The mute sympathy shown by the two as they stood near by calls out His responsive sympathy, and He binds them together in a new relationship for their mutual comfort and support. Christ establishes this close kinship, He whose earliest thought was of His home duties; He thinks in His last hour of His mother, and gives her into the safe-keeping of His friend.

Is it not a consolation to us that when the Son of God became Man, it was as the Son of Man? He entered into the world along the beaten track, taking His place as a child in the family, as a patriot in the nation, exhibiting to us how to live in the common relations of daily life. He was subject to his parents in the humble life of the Nazareth home. Of Jewish blood, He confined His labours to His own country and people, only touching incidentally the vast world beyond. By deliberate choice He limited the range of His human experience, and through the narrowness of the conditions into which He thus entered, He reached the widest possible sweep.

1. From the manger to the Cross He declares to us the sanctity and opportunity of family life. Cherish therefore the ties of

home. They are the greatest and grandest
things in the world. When they are broken
by the inevitable separations that are the
common lot, by calls to far-off duty and by
the stern summons of death, you will look
back with aching heart on the occasions you
let slip of being tender and of anticipating
the wants of those you love. God gives you
a holy trust; accept it, and faithfully meet
its obligations; realize your blessings now
while they are in your control. The time
will come when you will have only a memory of home life. May it be a happy one!
For you cannot reclaim the past; the opportunity that through selfishness, or indiffer-
ence, or thoughtlessness has slipped away is
gone forever. There is no pang keener than
that of mourning neglected opportunities of
tenderness at home. To those of us from
whom the opportunity has gone it is only
left to pray God to open another hereafter,
that in the higher life we may spring to fulfil
the duty left undone here. It is a consolation
to think that we may be permitted beyond
the grave to serve first of all those whom
we wounded or neglected here on earth.

2. For thirty years our Lord counted the home a large enough sphere for His activities. When He ceased to live in the family and to serve it, He served that development of the family which we call the nation.

Two things lay a supreme claim upon us, the family and the nation, the latter being second only to the former: the nation is but the family writ large. That which corresponds to filial love in the home is termed patriotism in the nation. The one leads to the other. The best citizens are the truest sons. Now Christ was a patriot. Look at His title as He hangs on the cross: " JESUS OF NAZARETH, THE KING OF THE JEWS." To the last He served the lost sheep of the house of Israel, though He longed to touch with compassionate hand the yearning Gentile world. So loyal was He to the people of His blood that, in spite of the fact that His self-chosen title, the Son of Man, indicated His relation to all mankind, His followers strove to claim Him as the special property of a few. St. Paul spent a lifetime trying to make men realize that Jew and Greek, bond and free, had equal rights,

Christ's Love of Home and Nation

equal claims, in Christ Jesus. It was hard for them to understand how one could be loyal to one's own nation without despising other nations.

Christ was indeed the universal man. He alone had the right to say, " My country is the world, and all mankind my country-men." But He claimed this right by means of home and country. At the beginning you can best, you can only, serve your country by serving your family; then later you will awake to the gladness of serving the world by being a loyal citizen of your country. Two characteristics marked our Lord's patriotism and separated it from what had gone before, lifting all patriotism to a new level of beauty and perfection. (*a*) His love of His own nation was illustrative of His love for all peoples as well as the means of creating and maintaining it. (*b*) He loved the Jews not for what they had been or were, but for what they were capable of becoming and ought to be.

(*a*) Christ's national love was not exclusive. The Jew of old emphasized his love for his own race by an uncompromising ha-

tred of the outside world. Whereas Christ's
love of His chosen people was an index tell-
ing of His love for the whole human race
of every kindred and tongue. In our day we
need such a pattern of patriotism, for the
old Jewish spirit lingers. National self-ap-
plause is as ill-bred and vulgar as personal
conceit,—and doubly so when the deficiencies of other countries are exhibited as a foil
for our own imagined perfection. Spread-
eagleism is a sin as well as a vulgarity.
Amongst us, too, frequently it is consid-
ered necessary to hate a competitive nation
or to foster those race prejudices, the roots
of which are buried deep in the past, in order to display what we deem an adequate
degree of patriotism. Never was there a
more deadly or dangerous fallacy. Just as
well might we argue that in order to exhibit
filial love and true devotion to our family,
it behooves us to hate every other family
in town. The law of equal love applies to the
broad stretches of life as exactingly as in
personal ethics. It is a principle of profound
importance that we should love our neighbour nations as ourselves; that we should

render them rich service, when necessity requires at cost to ourselves. It is not the "peace conference" or the amenities of diplomatic relations that will bind together all nations in unity and concord, but rather the growth of that higher patriotism that learns to look with disinterested eyes on the concerns of other countries as though they were its own, that would blush to secure an advantage for itself at the cost of wounding the life of a foreign state, that would not hesitate to be generous to a people in weakness and need, be the sacrifice that is entailed never so great. When the common people, who are the nation, foster the spirit of international sympathy, then, and only then, can we hope for international peace.

(b) Again, Christ's patriotism protested against the slavish adherence to tradition that coiled around the Jewish nation until its deepest life was extinct. He coveted for His people freedom, daring in ventures untried, in fields unwon. We know how in Church life the letter killeth. It is equally true in the life of the State. If the literal use of the Bible means death to the Spirit, much more does

[31]

the literal use of the greatest Constitution
ever framed involve death to the State that
gave it birth. Better were it to have no Constitution than to have a good one and to worship it. The Magi without a Bible were richer
than the Pharisees with the law and the prophets. Christian patriotism reverences the
past, but tunes its life to the future. It lingers
fondly over its traditions; but will not con-
sent to become a slave to them. It meets present needs with conscience and mind alert
to use what the situation demands. Some
of our most prominent statesmen trusted
the written Constitution, but not the government of and by the people: they trusted
the men of yesterday and their work, but
not those of their own generation. That is,
they believed in and loved their country for
what it had been and not for what it might
become. True patriotism believes that God
holds the nation in His hand to-day not less
than yesterday, and guides and controls its
destiny from moment to moment. When
clouds of national misfortune lower, when
novel and grave perplexities vex the soul,
when the ship of State is called upon to set its

sails in foreign seas, it is then that the true
patriot trusts his fellow citizens most, and
holds himself ready according to his capacity and opportunity to serve his country
with willing hands and hopeful heart. Christ
peers into the souls of men, even into the
darkest corners, and draws pearls therefrom:
in the Samaritan woman, in publicans and
sinners, He discerns potential saintliness. At
the darkest moment in Jewish national history he perceives its greatest opportunity.
He has ever in His mind what they may become, the spiritual masters of the world. It is
only on the eve of His death that He shuts
the door of opportunity to His nation when
it refuses His last offer. The Jews prefer selfish exclusiveness to universal service. Their
self-chosen penalty is national disintegra-
tion and conspicuous impotence, — the ulti-
mate doom of every self-centred nation.

May God plant deep family affection and
Christian patriotism in our land, so that we
may love not merely with our emotions, but
with our energies, and see and use all our
opportunities in home and State. May those
who are already active aspire to a still wider

reach of filial and patriotic love toward which to move.

Let us pray for our families and for our Nation.

AT the cross her station keeping
    Stood the mournful mother weeping,
Where He hung, the dying Lord;
For her soul of joy bereavèd,
Bowed with anguish deeply grievèd,
    Felt the sharp and piercing sword.

Oh, how sad and sore distressèd
Now was she, that mother blessèd
    Of the sole-begotten One;
Deep the woe of her affliction,
When she saw the crucifixion
    Of her ever-glorious Son.

Who, on Christ's dear mother gazing,
Pierced by anguish so amazing,
    Born of woman, would not weep?
Who, on Christ's dear mother thinking,
Such a cup of sorrow drinking,
    Would not share her sorrows deep?

For His people's sins chastisèd,
She beheld her Son despisèd,
    Scourged, and crowned with thorns
      entwined;

Christ's Love of Home and Nation

Saw Him then from judgment taken,
And in death by all forsaken,
    Till His spirit He resigned.

Jesu, may her deep devotion
Stir in me the same emotion,
    Fount of love, Redeemer kind;
That my heart fresh ardor gaining,
And a purer love attaining,
    May with Thee acceptance find.

SILENT PRAYER

GRANT, *O Lord, that whosoever are joined together in the holy estate of Matrimony, may faithfully perform and keep the vow and covenant between
them made, and may remain in perfect love together
unto their lives' end.*

O LORD, *our heavenly Father, the high and mighty
Ruler of the universe, who dost from thy throne
behold all the dwellers upon earth; Most heartily we
beseech thee, with thy favour to behold and bless thy servant* The President of the United States, *and all
others in authority; and so replenish them with the grace
of thy Holy Spirit, that they may always incline to thy
will, and walk in thy way. Endue them plenteously
with heavenly gifts; grant them in health and pro-
sperity long to live; and finally, after this life, to attain
everlasting joy and felicity; through Jesus Christ our
Lord.*

[35]

IV

The Consolation of
The Atonement

My God, my God, why didst Thou forsake Me?
S. Matt. xxvii, 46.[1]

WE can only approach to an understanding of this word. A deep darkness has fallen upon the land. Nature, herself a suffering thing, is used to suffering.
But before this spectacle of hideous misunderstanding, cruelty and injustice, she veils
herself in darkness, as though to emphasize
the sorrowful fact that the only unsympa-
thetic creature when the Son of God was dying, was man, made in God's image, His son.

During the hours in which the sun with-
held his shining, Christ's soul was clouded
as never before in His experience. This is not
the first time that depression and sorrow of
spirit have laid a heavy hand on Him. He has
been always a man of sorrows and acquaint-
ed with grief. He has explored almost with
eagerness the darkest corners of human experience, and fought those spiritual enemies

[1] *Margin, R. V.*

[37]

which try to destroy life with the weapons
of discouragement, trepitude and despair.
On each occasion—in the wilderness, on the
mountain top, in Gethsemane—He has conquered. Now the victories of the past rise up
to bless Him and to come to His rescue, as
deep waters engulf Him and the flood swal-
lows Him up. For three hours—the kind of
hours that must have seemed like centuries
—He waited for the storm that bowed his
soul to hell to sweep by, trusting that sooner
or later the light of heaven would come to
His relief. But not until he was on the very
verge of death did the clouds break, as a cry
that was at once the means and token of his
release, a wondering, pained cry, pierced
heaven: "My God, my God, why didst
Thou forsake Me?" In its presence the human mind at first is shocked—is this a fit-
ting cry for the lips of God's Son?—then
baffled; but at last our eyes become accus-
tomed to the gloom that shrouds the mystery and we see a part, only a part, yet enough
to make us bow our heads in reverence before it.

   This strange exclamation of the dying

The Atonement

Lord tells us that the purest life is not exempt from the most devastating inner grief, and that spiritual conflict thickens with advancing years. We must not fall into the mistake of thinking that after a while we will fight our way clear, that the toil of the upward climb will cease while life on earth lasts. From first to last we must be warriors; the road winds up the hill all the way, nor is it any mark of displeasure on the part of God toward us if our bitterest experiences come toward the end of our mortal career. Doubt, depression, fear, may hedge us in at any moment and rob us of that joyous freedom that we claim as our Christian heritage. Christ did nothing to merit punishment, but because He entered the human family and lived in accord with God's will He was wounded with our stripes, and the moment of His supreme triumph was a moment of shadows and suffering. Our destiny cannot be essentially different from His, for He is our elder brother. He lived the sample Christian life. It must be quieting to our anxieties when we approach some fresh trouble to remember that He went through it all

and came out unscathed—nay, came out
with the honour and glory that He found
lying hidden beneath the shadows which
enfolded Him. If toward the close of life
joy flies, if we seem to break away from our
anchorage and are tossed by seething waves
on an untried sea, we shall find consolation in the knowledge that we are sharing
Christ's experience, with whom all was well
when all seemed lost. The mystery of lives
shattered in their prime by disease or dis-
aster is solved by the character of Christ's
last experiences.

Sayest thou then to all who will to hearken —
'The saint's star grows not dim,
'But still through clouds that climb and deeps that
   darken
'Is visible to him, —

'Still when the sunset comes, He *taketh order*
'To whom the right belongs
'To send His own away across the border
'Silverly and with songs'?

Nay! God prepares His Kings for coronation
Not as might you or I,
And being wondrous, works His preparation
For Kingship wondrously.

[40]

The Atonement

Not always in the triumph of the sainting
That which our hearts expect.
Tearfully, roughly, doubtingly, and fainting,
How many saints elect

Pass out from hence within the lifted curtain; —
Roughly into the smooth,
Doubtfully into the forever certain,
The circumfulgent truth!

Tearfully, tearfully, becoming tearless
When trouble's all but o'er,
Fainting when well they might at last be fearless
Seeing they touch the shore;

Questioning hard by the school unemulous
Where half our questions cease,
Scarcely a bowshot off their beds, and tremulous
Upon the verge of peace,

Head drooping just before the crown is fitted,
Eyes dim at break of day,
Feet walking feebly through the meadows wetted
With April—into May.[1]

Those three hours of gloom-bound silence
were hours of spiritual conflict. Faith was
exercising its highest function, clinging to

[1] *Tenebræ, by Archbishop Alexander.*

The Consolation of

God unaided by any other faculty. As an arm of fire striking across an Egyptian night the releasing cry went forth. It was the final blow in a royal battle.

You and I live our lives only for half they are worth. "Man partly is and wholly hopes to be." When Jesus came to live as man, He lived it so thoroughly that he touched it at its farthest boundary. Its heights and its depths were explored so that when He had finished there was nothing left to endure, nothing to discover. His pain, like his joy, is not to be understood because He alone of the human race went through it. We can truly know only what we have gone through: community of experience is necessary for perfect sympathy. During those hours of darkness Christ was in a purgatory of pain — our purgatory into which He, without spot or blemish, entered, cleansing us. "With His stripes we are healed." At that moment the full weight of human sin, sin that was not His own and yet for that very reason all the more His own, pressed His soul down into hell.

Christ was a sin-bearer from the begin-

[42]

ning. We can see the process dimly. At first
as a gentle, spotless child, just waking to
consciousness, He saw the small deficiencies in the home life, for there were no char-
acters in the family at Nazareth save His
that were not more or less incomplete and
faulty. Do you remember the first time you
were compelled to look upon the sin of a
companion, such a sin as you had not even
dreamed of? Oh, the shame, the pain of it!
You feel it now as you recall that long distant experience. It seemed as though it were
your own sin; it clung to you and defiled
you; it disturbed your dreams and greeted
you in the morning as a mountain of sorrow — you had no idea that the world could
be so wicked.

Well, this was what Christ went through,
for He was in all points like as we are, actual sin excepted. His was the ordinary experience of life: little by little He came into touch with the vices and crimes of men.
Each fresh revelation of shame made Him
more truly the Sin-bearer, for so great was
His sympathy, so sensitive His love, that
each sin rested on His soul as though it

had been His own. No wonder that He
joined the throng at Jordan and was baptized. His delicate conscience had the heav-
iest burden of all the multitude who sought
the Baptist's ministrations. A parent enters
into his child's public shame as if it were
his own — it *is* his own, though he is without guilt. The grief of it, the pain of it, is
more the father's than the son's. So we can
comprehend how Christ gathered into His
spotless life the sins of humanity; and the
consequence He accepts, — the hiding of
God's face. From experience too we understand how the evil-doing of others can dis-
turb our peace with God. Sometimes when
a dear one has gone far wrong, night de-
scends and the darkness is impenetrable: all
we can do is to trust and wait. Yes, after
all, that agonized cry from the Cross is not
shrouded in unintelligible mystery, a burden on the shoulders of naked faith: the
common human experience, His and ours,
leads us a short distance at least toward an
understanding of it.

When in penitence for sin our souls are
oppressed with a darkness that can change

wholesome sorrow into a diseased and morbid brooding, or when because of our repeated failures and disappointments we skirt
the valley of despair almost ready to give
up the fight, our hope is in the present
consolation and support of the Sin-bearer.
His sympathy abides; He knows the pain
of depression—is there any greater?—and
comforts us by ministering to our need out
of His own victorious, but at the same time
suffering experience. From the depths of
the abyss He sounded—the abyss of a
world's shame—He speaks to us. There is
no human grief so deep, no human pain so
extreme, that Christ does not speak up to
us as from a still more profound experience
of suffering. Sympathy never comes from
above, always from beneath : it knows the
whole story, and more. It is a rock that
rises to meet our sinking feet. What surer
word of cheer than that which says: "I
know it all: have been through it and more.
God did not fail me. Nor will He fail you
now." It is thus that the Victor's victory is
shared with others who are still in the thick
of the battle.

The Consolation of

What consolation then, I say, to know that Christ has endured to the very limit, that the world of evil has exhausted itself on Him to no purpose other than its own discomfiture! It has no weapon to wield that He has not shattered, no pain to inflict which He has not conquered by undergoing it, no woe to mete out that He has not enriched Himself from. Christ has stored up a wealth of sympathy commensurate with human need, so that we can afford to wait, at least without dismay or confusion, even in the presence of seeming abandonment. "O Lord, in Thee have I trusted: let me never be confounded."

Let us pray that God will sustain us, console us, rescue us in those hours of depression and loneliness that may be ahead of us. Let us pray for our fellows whose lives are clouded by doubt, perplexity and despair.

O SACRED Head surrounded
     By crown of piercing thorn!
O bleeding Head, so wounded,
     Reviled and put to scorn!
Death's pallid hue comes o'er Thee,
     The glow of life decays,

The Atonement

Yet angel-hosts adore Thee,
  And tremble as they gaze.

I see Thy strength and vigor,
  All fading in the strife,
And death with cruel rigor,
  Bereaving Thee of life;
O agony and dying!
  O love to sinners free!
Jesu, all grace supplying,
  Oh, turn Thy face on me.

In this, Thy bitter Passion,
  Good Shepherd, think of me
With Thy most sweet compassion,
  Unworthy though I be:
Beneath Thy cross abiding
  Forever would I rest,
In Thy dear love confiding,
  And with Thy presence blest.

Be near when I am dying;
  Oh, show Thy cross to me:
And to my succor flying,
  Come, Lord, and set me free.
These eyes, new faith receiving,
  From Jesus shall not move;
For he, who dies believing,
  Dies safely through Thy love.

SILENT PRAYER

The Atonement

O UT *of the deep have I called unto thee, O Lord:
Lord, hear my voice.*

O let thine ears consider well the voice of my complaint.

If thou, Lord, wilt be extreme to mark what is done amiss, O Lord, who may abide it?

For there is mercy with thee; therefore shalt thou be feared.

I look for the Lord; my soul doth wait for him; in his word is my trust.

My soul fleeth unto the Lord, before the morning watch; I say, before the morning watch.

O Israel, trust in the Lord; for with the Lord there is mercy, and with him is plenteous redemption.

And he shall redeem Israel from all his sins.

I N *the midst of life we are in death; of whom may
we seek for succour, but of thee, O Lord, who for
our sins art justly displeased?*

*Yet, O Lord God most holy, O Lord most mighty,
O holy and most merciful Saviour, deliver us not into the bitter pains of eternal death.*

*Thou knowest, Lord, the secrets of our hearts; shut
not thy merciful ears to our prayer; but spare us,
Lord most holy, O God most mighty, O holy and merciful Saviour, thou most worthy Judge eternal, suffer us not, at our last hour, for any pains of death,
to fall from thee.*

[48]

V
The Consolation of
Christ's Conquest of Pain

I thirst. S. JOHN xix, 25.

ONLY a few moments before death our
Lord thinks of bodily needs. A theo-
rist would say that on the verge of the grave,
the cravings of an exhausted and tortured
nature would be of no account to a righteous man. His mind would be set on the new
day that was about to dawn: he would probably ignore the last demands of the physical
part of his being for momentary relief. That
is theory. The fact is that when the Son of
Righteousness was deep in the valley of the
shadow, He held His body to be an integral
portion of His personality, to be attended to
and cared for in its legitimate demands.

How this contradicts the contention of
certain modern idealists who maintain that
the body is ultimately of no account, that it
is to the true self only what a glove is to the
hand, that its troubles are figments of the
imagination, and that there is no resurrection of the flesh!

But it is neither by ignoring the body and relegating it with its aches and pains to the category of things unreal, nor by "medical materialism" throwing our full weight on the triumphs of science, that we can best combat physical ills and achieve physical well-being. When faith accepts science and science accepts faith, each viewing the other as a potent force over disease, there will be won such victories over sickness and frailty as to-day are only happy dreams. The human body, as our Lord attests, is a holy thing; it is a necessary part of personality, here and hereafter; without it man is not wholly man. It has its legitimate needs here,—needs which must be ministered to up to the last.

How truly human is our Lord! He is the Son of God, but also and just as completely the Son of Man. He is susceptible to all human experience — His soul to anguish through others' sins, His mind to the lashings (though impotent) of doubt, His body to pain. He is natural, *i.e.* He acts out human life under human conditions to the very end, and responds to the innocent cravings of His flesh. "I thirst." He refused the

[50]

draught that would benumb His faculties,
but looked and gently asked for relief in His
fierce thirst. And in so doing He excites us
to a new recognition of the duty of helping
physical need in our fellows. His cry awoke
quick-footed Pity, who with fertile energy
fixed the wetted sponge to the reed and
sprang to his succour. Mary and John have
bathed His human soul in the refreshing
stream of their sympathy; and now His im-
plied request for something to relieve His
parched lips, brings a response from an unknown, unnamed friend. Let us fill in the
hiatus and give him a worthy name; let it
be Human Compassion.

Our Lord's thirst stands as the symbol of
the whole realm of pain. Thirst was the typ-
ical pain of the Cross; and in that the Cross
was chosen by Christ to be His portion, this
torturing thirst was part of His voluntary
suffering.

There are two kinds of pain in human
experience, the pain that is inevitable and
the pain that is chosen. First there is the
unerring, exacting, unavoidable suffering
which you cannot escape. However cunning

or fleet-footed you may be, sooner or later bereavement, sickness, death will come: it will arrive when it is due; each dark-visaged assailant is a plain fact of a rational universe, and must be seriously reckoned with. You must become either its victim or its victor; if you fail to face and conquer it to the enrichment of your character, it will harden and impoverish your soul. It is difficult to bear pain of any sort, and as I think of the days of suffering which lie ahead, I know that unless God abides with me, when the storm breaks I shall perish.

But the pain which is most of all typified by the Cross and its characteristic torture of thirst is not the pain that is inevitable; rather is it that which is chosen. By this I do not mean that our Lord ever chose suffering because it was suffering, as though it had some inherent virtue, or as though the Father found delight in the spectacle of one of His creatures in pain. What He did do was to lay His life along a course which, if it led to a lofty goal, led to it by the ladder of the Cross. Whenever a man chooses something high, he chooses a cross. Because

Christ's Conquest of Pain

Christ chose the highest vocation, the vocation of Saviour, at the same time He chose *the* Cross, *i.e.* the hardest cross that the world can know. He knew the cost which His choice involved; He knew that if he was to save others, Himself He could not save. The pain of the Saviour was the pain which only refined, sensitive natures can experience. Capacity for righteousness or for service entails capacity for suffering; and the higher you rise the larger the capacity, until you reach the perfection of our Lord, which touches the outermost bounds of human possibility.

Now it is fatally easy to avoid the pain which is typified by the Cross. He who keeps his nature coarse, defending it from refining influences, will move serenely, smilingly through stretches of life which a highly developed character can traverse only at the cost of bleeding feet and shuddering soul. The impenitent robber plunged hilariously, blasphemingly into the pain that helped to break the heart of the Saviour. The soul that claims for itself the refinements of the Incarnation, that not merely tries to avoid what is wrong, but to discern between the good and the less good, that searches daily for new and hitherto unrevealed aspects of Christian living,—such a soul *ipso facto* courts the pain of the Cross. Every call to Christ is a call to suffering. It must be so. God has erected crosses between us and the ideal to keep desecrating, unprepared hands from soiling the prize or misusing it, as we surely would if we grasped it too early. But each seeming obstacle proves to be an aid if we are patient, and by its help we mount to the joy and freedom of the ideal.

What a consolation that Christ was so truly one with us, that He, too, "though he was a Son, yet learned obedience by the things which he suffered!" We would have a right to conclude that we had made some fatal mistake when, after trying to do right, we were to meet with nothing but rebuffs and failure, were it not that the Son of God has acted out before our eyes the complete experience, and taught us how we court pain when we woo an ideal. Not a few fall by the wayside because they have never learned this elementary lesson of Christianity. We

are caught in the splendour of some vision;
we spring to claim it for our own, and immediately a hostile army confronts us.

> *Where we looked for crowns to fall*
> *We find the tug's to come, — that's all.*

At such a moment we need the experience
of our Lord to lean upon. The servant
ought to be content to be as his Master.
Our consolation is that if every call to Christ
and his righteousness is a call to suffering,
the converse is equally true—every call to
suffering is a call to Christ, a promotion, an
invitation to come up higher.

Let us then be brave Christians, not faltering before new pain, not turned aside because the Cross blocks the way to achievement; for the call to suffer is a call to win
as well. "The God of all grace, who called
you unto his eternal glory in Christ, after
that ye have suffered a little while, shall
himself perfect, stablish, strengthen you.
To him be the dominion for ever and ever.
Amen." Let us pray for all sufferers in
mind, body or estate; especially for those
who are suffering for righteousness' sake,

and for such as are striving to set up new
and ever higher standards.

ART thou weary, art thou languid,
  Art thou sore distrest?
"Come to Me," saith One, "and coming,
  Be at rest."

Hath He marks to lead me to Him,
  If He be my guide?
"In His feet and hands are wound-prints,
  And His side."

Is there diadem, as monarch,
  That His brow adorns?
"Yea, a crown, in very surety,
  But of thorns."

If I find Him, if I follow,
  What His guerdon here?
"Many a sorrow, many a labor,
  Many a tear."

If I still hold closely to Him,
  What hath He at last?
"Sorrow vanquished, labor ended,
  Jordan past."

If I ask Him to receive me,
  Will He say me nay?
"Not till earth, and not till heaven
  Pass away."

Christ's Conquest of Pain

Finding, following, keeping, struggling,
    Is He sure to bless?
Saints, apostles, prophets, martyrs,
    Answer, " Yes."

SILENT PRAYER

THAT *it may please thee to succour, help, and comfort, all who are in danger, necessity, and tribulation;*
    We beseech thee to hear us, good Lord.

That it may please thee to preserve all who travel by land or by water, all women in the perils of childbirth, all sick persons, and young children; and to show thy pity upon all prisoners and captives;
    We beseech thee to hear us, good Lord.

That it may please thee to defend, and provide for, the fatherless children, and widows, and all who are desolate and oppressed;
    We beseech thee to hear us, good Lord.

WE *humbly beseech thee, O Father, mercifully to look upon our infirmities; and, for the glory of thy Name, turn from us all those evils that we most justly have deserved; and grant, that in all our troubles we may put our whole trust and confidence in thy mercy, and evermore serve thee in holiness and pureness of living, to thy honour and glory; through our only Mediator and Advocate, Jesus Christ our Lord.*

Cfie Consolation of
Christ's Completeness

It is finished. S. JOHN xix, 30.

THIS is not a cry of relief, but of joy.
The Word is expressive of that spiritual gladness whose flame burns brightest
oftentimes when adversity is the companion
of our bosom. Life is not all pain; joys are
scattered up and down the whole of life's
pathway. Enduring joy will shine out even
in the shadow of the Cross. If our Lord
speaks of losing life for His sake and the
Gospel's, in the same breath He speaks
also of keeping it to life eternal. He who has
learned his lesson aright turns the full flood
of suffering as it comes to him upon the
meaner, lower part of his nature; in so doing
he relieves the higher part so that it at once rejoices in a larger freedom. The higher is glad
because the lower has been made sorry. You
cannot discipline your actual self without
caressing your ideal self. So it happens that
side by side with the cry of pain comes the
cry of triumph: "I thirst"—"It is finished."

He does not say: "It is ended; it is all
over and I am relieved." But after having
scanned His career with that infallible accu-
racy which belongs to the last hours of consciousness, His verdict is that everything
has been done that was to be done. The
purpose of His life has been achieved. Can
you conceive of any fuller gladness than
that? His first recorded word is that He
must be busy about the things of His
Father. As a little lad He set His purpose
before His face, and in after life He never
wavered. To do God's will was His duty,
—that which He was bound to do; and His
meat,—that which He was hungry to do. So
that now when the splendour of it rushes like
a flood of sunlight into His soul, He rises
to a joy comparable to that of the Transfigu-
ration when, for the moment, the beauty
hid the pain of self-sacrifice. Once again, at
the close of life, when pain's last blow has
been delivered and His every faculty is
shivering under its shock, joy bursts in triumphant. This is the joy which, when it
becomes our portion, no man taketh from
us even though the shield, the sword, and

the battle try to rob us with merciless as-
saults. It is the joy that comes direct from
and is held in place by the hand of God.
Our Lord's life, which began with the joy
of boundless promise, closed with the joy
of promise fulfilled.

It is hard to conceive of a work that is so
far above criticism as to be flawless in the
sight of God. Only the self-sufficient are
fully satisfied as they view a concluded task.
The talented and great always see a gulf between what they strove to do and what they
really accomplished. Herbert Spencer's pa-
thetic preface to the last volume of his "Syn-
thetic Philosophy" is an illustration of this.
"At length," he says, "the end is reached.
Doubtless in earlier days some exultation
would have resulted; but as age creeps on
feelings weaken, and now my chief pleasure
is in my emancipation. Still there is satisfaction in the consciousness that losses, dis-
couragements, and shattered health have not
prevented me from fulfilling the purpose of
my life."

He ended, he did not finish his work;
and the only solace that came to him was

The Consolation of

the satisfaction due to loyalty to his early purpose.

This is what will happen to you and to me. Our lives are incomplete now, and at best will be relatively but little more complete when we come to die. If we develop in character we shall realize more acutely then than now the immensity of our deficiencies. Where can we turn for comfort but to Him who fulfilled His duty to the last jot and tittle? Out of the abundance of His completeness we can draw to fill up what is lacking in us. If it is consequent on the unity of life that the sin of one can taint a whole race, it is equally true that the righteousness of One can vitalize the world of men, that the perfection of One can complete all. He stands by each one of us at our life's task as a master workman stands beside his pupils. A touch here and another there from His hand makes all the difference between completeness and incompleteness.

A while since an afflicted friend sent me one of those home-made tokens of affection that are valuable above gold and silver. "Here," she said, "is a bit of sea-weed I ga-

Christ's Completeness

thered some few years back — a bit of God's work which I send as an Easter greeting. Humble enough as far as my own part in it goes, but — God did the rest." Man's little and God's much hand in hand, the wonder and the magnitude of the latter more than compensating for the modest proportions of the former! What consolation to know that it is part of God's joy *to do the rest* when we have done our best. Through and in Him we make real *the duty up to its ideal.* Lying behind that measure of success which we are capable of achieving must be the same directive and motive power that enabled our Lord to say at the end, "It is finished." We must know God's will and do it. What is God's will concerning you? What does God mean you to do that no one else can do? Find out — first in the large, and then day by day in detail. You have gifts of opportunity, of talent, of capacity for service which cannot be duplicated, any more than a leaf from yonder tree can have its perfect counterpart. Your first duty is to ask God what He wants of you and your endowments.

But how are we to find out? The voices

that speak within are numerous, confusing, and even contradictory. The only way to discover is to ask God. He is a Father, and a father will not refuse to tell that which most of all he desires his child to know. I do not say this in the spirit of reckless mysticism that creates a visionary, impractical character. I am profoundly conscious of the difficulty of ascertaining God's will; in its more delicate shadings, after we mount above the broad field of common morals and face the uplands of the spiritual life, it is far harder to discern it than to do it when it has disclosed itself. But, to change the simile, the little shallop of human personality was made to float on the great sea of God's eternal purpose. It is safe nowhere else. If we patiently trim our sails, in due time the breath of God's Spirit will lay its firm but gentle pressure upon them, and waft us along the course of our appointed destiny. I am disposed to think that the common fault consists not in the failure of men to ask God to reveal His will, but in their almost total neglect to listen in stillness for His answer. Times without number men do God's will, but they are unaware of it; for they have not taken the trouble to ascertain whether their lives are attuned to Him or not. The result is that they are devoid of that peculiar joy and peace, to say nothing of the power, which accompany the consciousness of working under His immediate direction. Efficiency is contingent upon some sense of vocation at any rate.

Is it not a consolation to us who desire to know and to do God's will that our Elder Brother, although having seasons of dimness when He could not clearly discern His path, as for example in Gethsemane, was never without sufficient light. Like Him we are bound to have moments when innocent desire, which seems to lead close to His throne, will be held in check by some mighty inner impulse which apparently leads into the dark. Nor will the issue of the struggle be doubtful if our set purpose, like His, is to respond to the will of God. If for a time we lose the light in our search for it, it will only be that we may find it again with greater brilliancy. So again I say: Seek for God's will in season and out of season, that you may

do a work that is like in intention to that
of the Saviour. Only thus can its cracks and
flaws be filled in by the completeness of His.

> *So, take and use Thy work:*
> *Amend what flaws may lurk,*
> *What strain o' the stuff, what warpings*
>   *past the aim!*

> *My times be in Thy hand!*
> *Perfect the cup as planned!*
> *Let age approve of youth, and death com-*
>   *plete the same.*

Let us pray for wisdom to see God's will,
and power to do the same till the day breaks
and faith gives place to sight, weakness to
strength.

OFT in danger, oft in woe,
    Onward, Christians, onward go:
Fight the fight, maintain the strife,
Strengthened with the Bread of life.

Let your drooping hearts be glad:
March in heavenly armor clad:
Fight, nor think the battle long,
Soon shall victory tune your song.

Let not sorrow dim your eye,
Soon shall every tear be dry;

Christ's Completeness

Let not fears your course impede,
Great your strength, if great your need.

Onward then to battle move,
More than conquerors ye shall prove;
Though opposed by many a foe,
Christian soldiers, onward go.

SILENT PRAYER

ALMIGHTY *and merciful God, of whose only gift
it cometh that thy faithful people do unto thee
true and laudable service; Grant, we beseech thee, that
we may so faithfully serve thee in this life, that we fail
not finally to attain thy heavenly promises; through the
merits of Jesus Christ our Lord.*

VII

⚔️he Consolation of Death's Conquest

Father, into thy hands I commend my spirit.

S. LUKE xxiii, 46.

WITH this sweet cadence the mortal
life of our Redeemer comes to its
close. The storm has subsided and a hush
falls on land and sea. Human passion and
the army of evil have done their worst; their
waves have lashed *that Rock* with final fury,
and now fall back baffled and lifeless. Death
leaps to the assault only to spill the soul of
the Son of Man into the lap of God. At the
moment of sunset the Word of duty melts
into the Word of trust: "Father, into thy
hands I commend my spirit."

"No man who is not a brute can say that
he is not afraid of death," said a dying states-
man.[1] Even Christ feared. He made no com-
pact with man's arch-enemy; He conquered
it as the last onslaught of sin. Death, whether then or now, is always a foe and will remain so until it has been destroyed. "The last

[1] *Daniel Webster.*

[69]

enemy that shall be destroyed is death." Our Lord "abolished death" only in the sense of extracting its sting. Death will cease to be when there are no more to die, when it will no longer have dominion over man in the same manner and for the same reason that it has none over Christ.

What was it that carried the Saviour through this last experience? It was trust in God. He laid Himself in the sustaining arms of the Father, as a little child nestles to its mother's bosom, whispering words of confidence and peace. "Trust in God is the last of all things and the whole of all things." God always, is the complete history of Jesus. He came from God, lived in God, and went to God. He who had trusted that He would have light to see and power to do God's will, trusted to the end, and He met with no disappointments. When men strive to do God's will there is nothing that can bring the kind of disappointment that sears the heart and paralyzes the vitality. In Browning's description of the life of Lazarus after his resurrection, this is well portrayed: —

Death's Conquest

The especial marking of the man
Is prone submission to the heavenly will.

. . . .

He will live, nay, it pleaseth him to live
So long as God please and just how God please.
He even seeketh not to please God more
(Which meaneth, otherwise) than as God please.

Upon the return of Lazarus to this world, he was fired with a consuming trust. Nothing could quench it; nothing dim its flame. Trust had been tested to the limit, and there had been no disappointment.

So may it be with us. The rough places which day by day bruise the feet of men can be endured if we believe that we are but treading the same path once trod victoriously by Sacred Feet, that we are being led by a pierced but unerring Hand; and we must early strive to come to an experimental knowledge of this truth. We can be trained in the Christian grace of trust only in the common occurrences of life. A great task lies ahead for trust to perform. Trust's last work on earth is to carry us through the valley of the shadow of death, when sunset comes. But it is in the morning of life, when

[71]

the pulse beats full and strong, that we must learn to lay ourselves quietly, without fear, on his broad, brave wings, so that we may be well practised when the last hard flight that is to carry us through the portals of death, is before us.

This was not the first time that Christ's lips had framed the prayer of trust. He was skilled in the exercise. Each day had begun with the same self-surrender. He trusted in God that He would deliver Him in His boyhood trials, in the heat of manhood's temptation, in the pain of misunderstanding and persecution — in short from the manger to the Cross. His reward is that now, when He can do naught for Himself, but must leave all things to the Father, it is no effort for Him to trust. He does it intuitively. There was a day, before the night had come in which no man can work, when the promptings of evil had urged Him to trust, and only trust, though His arms were free to toil. "He shall give his angels charge over thee, that thou dash not thy foot against a stone." But it was a false trust to which Satan challenged Him on the dizzy height of the Temple's

Death's Conquest

pinnacle;—not trust at all, but insolent assurance. Now the arms that had been so active are transfixed, the feet so swift in mercy
have made their last journey, the heart of
love so sensitive to others' woe is broken.
He does the only thing that remains for
Him to do: He trusts. And because He has
trusted at the beginning and in the middle
of His career, because He has trusted in
His activity, He now trusts triumphantly,
gloriously, at the end.

Am I wrong in thinking that self-trust
is to an unusual degree the sin of the age?
Civilization has strewn the path of progress
with the spoils of science and the fruits of
invention. Discomfort is reduced to a min-
imum, distance has been conquered, disease
is increasingly within our power. Humanity
is crowned with the diadem of intellectual
conquest and material success, and the heart
is swollen with pride. Just how much we
lean on temporal supports, only those know
who in wholesome self-discipline for a season have tried to live without them, or from
whose lives the pitiless hand of adversity
has swept them. By some strange self-de-

lusion men and women whose whole weight is thrown upon things material, if they think of the end at all, seem to find satisfaction in considering the trust by which they will then be sustained. Weak sentimentalism fostering a false hope! How shall we be able to trust God in great things, if we have never had enough faith to trust Him in small things? How shall we have any confidence at the hour of death in One whose love and power we have never allowed ourselves to experience in life? Our money, our genius, our luck, our ideas, our plans, carried us through life. God was not in our thoughts. Believe me, there will come a day when "the cord is frayed and the cruse is dry." There will be nothing left for us to do but trust; and what if we find ourselves without the capacity of faith? The shadows of death will try the temper of our life, of what sort it is —our motives, our ambitions, our belief in God's personal providence. As far as we are concerned the foundations of the firmament will be broken up. Then will it be made evident to whom we have given the glory, whether to God or to self. No self-confidence can carry us through death,—nothing but the power of God evoked by trust on our part.

To-day is the hour in which to learn the lesson of trust. What comfort to know that the Life which was lived wholly in the atmosphere of trust was the only complete life in human history! What gladness and encouragement in the assurance that God has never once failed, not merely to respond to trust, but to surprise trust by giving beyond its fairest expectations! What peace to live in the knowledge that we need not worry about the terrors of death as we look ahead and anticipate our last hour; if we but trust now we shall be able to trust with a practised faith then, as Christ trusted, and there will be "light at evening time." Christ, who in Himself conquered death, will repeat His victory in us and for us.

Thus it is that in the Cross we find our sufficient consolation. Our faltering hearts grow brave as we contemplate Jesus of the Passion. What larger consolations can life hold than those revealed in the royal bequest of the Saviour's dying words? Here

they are once more, compressed into brief
compass: The largest hope is not denied the
worst; forgiveness is not merely a remission, but an admission,—yes, more than
an admission, a commission, to fellowship
with God in Christ; the home and the nation together with the Church form God's
triple throne on earth; Christ endured to
the limit, even to taking upon Him the sins
of the world; He went through the abyss of
pain that it might become to us the ladder
of achievement; in duty done is exultant
joy, even when suffering is at its height;
trust is victory, whether in life or in death.

O Love, I give myself to Thee,
Thine ever, only Thine, to be.

PEACE, perfect peace, in this dark world of
sin?
The blood of Jesus whispers peace within.

Peace, perfect peace, by thronging duties pressed?
To do the will of Jesus, this is rest.

Peace, perfect peace, with sorrows surging round?
On Jesus' bosom naught but calm is found.

Death's Conquest

Peace, perfect peace, with loved ones far away?
In Jesus' keeping we are safe, and they.

Peace, perfect peace, our future all unknown?
Jesus we know, and He is on the throne.

Peace, perfect peace, death shadowing us and ours?
Jesus has vanquished death and all its powers.

It is enough: earth's struggles soon shall cease,
And Jesus call us to heaven's perfect peace.

Let us pray for a Christian death
without sin, without shame,
and, should it please God, without pain,
and a good answer
at the dreadful and fearful judgment-seat
of Jesus Christ, our Lord.

SILENT PRAYER

GRANT, *O Lord, that as we are baptized into*
the death of thy blessed Son, our Saviour Jesus
Christ, so by continual mortifying our corrupt affec-
tions we may be buried with him; and that through
the grave, and gate of death, we may pass to our joyful
resurrection; for his merits, who died, and was buried,
and rose again for us, thy Son Jesus Christ our Lord.

[77]

Death's Conquest

THE God of peace, who brought again from the dead our Lord Jesus Christ, the great Shepherd of the sheep, through the blood of the everlasting covenant; Make you perfect in every good work to do his will, working in you that which is well pleasing in his sight; through Jesus Christ, to whom be glory for ever and ever. Amen.

TWO SERMONS

In Whom was no Guile[1]

Jesus saw Nathanael coming to him, and saith of him, Behold an Israelite indeed, in whom is no guile.

S. JOHN i. 47.

IT must have been a great joy to our Saviour to praise men who were worthy of praise — and He praised none who were not. His was an appreciative eye; His were appreciative lips. So He never failed to recognize the commendable character or even the commendable action, and to comment on it. Instances flock to the memory. Of John the Baptist He said, "Verily I say unto you, among them that are born of women there hath not arisen a greater than John the Baptist." "He was a burning and a shining light." Upon S. Peter He bestowed a rich benediction in recognition of the Apostle's spiritual discernment: "Blessed art thou, Simon Bar-Jona: . . . thou art Peter, and upon this rock I will build my church." Over the faith of the Roman official He marvelled, and declared He had "not found

[1] *Preached in memory of Henry Martyn Torbert, minister of S. Stephen's Church, Boston, on Sunday, October 6, 1901.*

[81]

In Whom was no Guile

so great faith, no, not in Israel." He commended Mary as having chosen that "good
part which shall not be taken away from
her." And in the case before us He declares
the sterling worth of Nathanael. He is a true
Israelite, one who is what the name implies
—a prince of God; one who is loyal to all
that is real in his nation and in the faith of
his fathers; a man in whom is no guile—
whose transparency of character is without
shadow, whose activities are but the reflec-
tion of his motives, the expression of his inner life.

Yes, it must have been a joy to the Son
of man when He walked on earth amidst its
woes and wickedness to discover and commend that which was praiseworthy. And
what was, shall be; that is to say, on the day
of judgement, when our career on earth will
have a final seal set upon it, it will be the
joy of the Judge to say again and again,
"Well done, good and faithful servant!"
The day of judgement will be an awful day;
but it will also be a day of joyous surprises
and of resounding song, a blest, a calm, a
bright, a glad day, because the Judge is

In Whom was no Guile

the Saviour, gentle, considerate, forgiving
—commending rather than condemning.
"Then shall every man have his praise of
God."

In between that yesterday of long ago
when Jesus gave such high praise to Nathanael as a character, and that to-morrow—
whether it be far or near God only knows—
when rewards will be set on the brows of
men who have been true to Christ, lies the
long stretch of time of which to-day is a
portion. And what of this period? Is Jesus
silent now except to censure sin? Is He re-
serving His words of praise and apprecia-
tion until the day of judgement? Did He
commend John the Baptist and S. Peter and
the rest as quite unique persons who stood
apart from all who came after? No, a thou-
sand times no. The commending Jesus of
yesterday and of to-morrow is the commending Jesus of to-day. An hour does not pass,
no, not a minute, in which He does not flash
His approval upon some child of earth;
and, believe me, it is the only reward in the
world worth seeking or keeping. Who has
not on some occasion heard Him say in the

In Whom was no Guile

depths of a peaceful conscience: "I know
thy works, thy patience, thy love, thy faith.
Be thou faithful unto death and I will give
thee a crown of life."

Yes, the Saviour loves to praise us to-day
when we strive to be and do and suffer according to His will. Those who, as we read
in Scripture, were commended by Him of
old stand as the representative types of
character which He always and everywhere
praises—the lowly, the faithful, the loving,
the guileless. Nor does ever a life close which
has been lived in His service that He fails
to reveal its worth to the eyes of those who
stand near by. With what dignity a completed life rises on our vision! Incidental
blemishes fade out, and we see character as
it is. God seems to repeat to us who remain
the judgement He pronounces in the ear of
the departed soul at the moment of death.
Men are more truly measured by their fellows when life closes than at any other time.
The trumpet-note of the Saviour's praise
echoes to earth and for the moment drowns
with its jubilance and beauty the petty criti-
cisms, the false and disproportionate judge-

ments that blind us to true human worth:
we hear in our souls the verdict of God, and
we cannot but admit that it is true.

This is something that all of us are feel-
ing to-day as the picture of that serene and
beloved face, with its noble brow, its honest eyes, its chaste mouth, rises to our memory. Somehow we know Henry Martyn
Torbert as never before. The Saviour has
pronounced upon him commending judgement, and in such vibrant tones as to allow
us to share the secret which will be eternal
joy to our dear brother. As to what Jesus
said to him and of him as he entered his
new home, there is no room for doubt. All
that day of tears and smiles that I spent in
the little Pennsylvania village where he once
lived, whether I was sitting in the refined
atmosphere of the home he loved, treading
the streets which so often had echoed to his
feet, kneeling by his side in the quiet church
where his body lay, or standing by the flower-
strewn grave, one sentence kept repeating
itself to me: " Behold an Israelite indeed,
in whom is no guile." This surely was the
greeting with which the Saviour welcomed

[85]

In Whom was no Guile

into Paradise his eager soul as it sped up
to Jesus' feet. For Henry Martyn Torbert
lived among us in the spirit and power of
Nathanael. To-day we are going to forget
our irreparable loss for a moment at any
rate, burying it in our exultation over the
completeness of life into which he has entered and the heritage that has been left us
in his enduring influence and example. And
in so doing we shall be taking the first step
toward making his spirit our own. In his
diary, which I shall quote freely in what I
am going to say, a diary composed mainly
of aspirations and spiritual reflections, there
is this entry made two days after his mother's
death and while her body was yet in the
house: "Mother said to me in the early part
of her illness, 'Do not grieve too much for
me'—therefore I am not to be unhappy
and I am not to be unchristian in my sorrow. I must try to regard all connected with
this change in the light with which she views
it in Paradise. I must live so that my sorrow can be *changed into* joy, not *followed by*
joy, because the impression will be lost in
time." And the day following he writes:

In Whom was no Guile

"I read the Gospels through the day to drink in the utterances of Christ on the Resurrection. . . . I must be happy through the grave and the Resurrection life." How fully he realized his purpose those of us know who were by his side during the days that followed. And we may not do less than he now that we are the mourners; so we surround ourselves with symbols of triumph and joy rather than those which bespeak grief. We deck our altar in white, adorning it with flowers: and we sing of the Communion of Saints, the Resurrection of the body, and the Life everlasting.

It is not so much the facts of his life that we want to think about just now as what he was in himself. But in order to reach a clear understanding of his character a brief sketch of his career will be serviceable. He was born in Upper Makefield, near Philadelphia, on December 2, 1845. His parents were devout adherents of the Presbyterian faith, and until his college days he was under the stern benignity of Calvinism. Serious illness retarded his studies as a boy and kept him from entering into youthful sports. His blameless

Jn Whom was no Guile

boyhood and a naturally religious tempera-
ment prepared him for that call to special
dedication which came to him with such
appealing force toward the end of his colle-
giate career. Though he entered Princeton
University he did not complete his course.
While there his interest in the Church was
ripened by surrounding influences to such
an extent that he embraced with zeal her
faith and eventually took holy orders.

Leaving Princeton he went to Trinity
College, Hartford, where he graduated in
1870, going thence to the General Theological Seminary for the prescribed course of
three years. His nature was one that could
find satisfaction only in the completest sur-
render to God, and his eyes were open for
opportunities to realize the life of absolute
consecration. During his seminary course
he became engrossed in the idea of community life, and thought he had found in
the English Society of S. John the Evangelist such an embodiment of his ideal as
he longed for. He was ordained deacon on
June 29, 1873, and proceeded immediately
to Oxford, where he was clothed as a novice

of the Cowley community on August 1,
1874. From first to last his life was one of
self-sacrifice, and what it cost a man of such
obviously domestic tastes and of so passion-
ately patriotic a spirit to enter English mo-
nastic life, cannot easily be measured. But
he did it as he did all, for the kingdom of
heaven's sake.

He left the community house in Cowley
without being professed as a member of the
order, owing to serious difficulties, mainly
in connection with the vows required. But
his loyalty to his original purpose kept him
more or less closely related to the Society
until the fall of the year 1891. His stability
was not the least feature of his character.

Upon his return to America he became
chaplain to the Sisters of S. Mary, Peekskill,
New York, in whose chapel at the House
of Mercy in New York City he had been
advanced to the priesthood on May 29,
1874. He left a deep impression on this community of devout women whom he served
from 1876 to 1883, when he joined the staff
of clergy at the Mission Church of S. John
the Evangelist, Boston. During his chap-

In Whom was no Guile

laincy in Peekskill he had free scope for the development of the reflective and devotional life which was always such a joy to him. With the Psalmist he could say: "Lord, what love have I unto Thy law: all the day long is my study in it." In after life he often referred to the spiritual happiness of that period. Upon coming to Boston he was more or less occupied in conducting missions and retreats in various parts of the country, as well as in doing parochial work.

When the Society recalled its provincial superior, Rev. A. C. A. Hall, in 1891, Mr. Torbert put himself in the hands of the Bishop of the diocese, Bishop Brooks, for such duty as might be allotted to him, and he was appointed to the newly purchased S. Stephen's Church, where work began shortly afterwards. The remainder of his career to the end has been a part of the life of most of you, and to all of us it is an inspiring and sacred memory.

Such, in brief, was the history of our Nathanael, "the gift of God"—for that is the meaning of Nathanael—to us for a season. He was an Israelite indeed; there was real-

In Whom was no Guile

ity corresponding to his profession. To his nation and his Church alike he was absolutely loyal.

He was an American indeed. His sense of responsibility as a citizen was uncommonly deep. Matters of national import were always of concern to him. I have seldom seen him angry in well-nigh fourteen years of hallowed and intimate fellowship with him; and never once have I known him to be unrighteously angry. It may be truthfully said of him as it was said of a man for whom he had profound admiration: At a "public crisis, as in many a private one, a fire of moral indignation would suddenly reveal itself in him which startled the ordinary man. We are used to such passion over personal wrongs; there it gives us no surprise. But a flame of righteous anger that has no trace of personal injury in it, and that leaps up at the sight of public wrong because it is wrong, and for no other reason—this is rare indeed. . . . Yet there it was. No one could mistake it. It was the pure, white anger of an outraged conscience. When once you had caught sight of it you never forgot it." On one occasion

In Whom was no Guile

I recall, he sternly rebuked, with words of flame, a young man who had wantonly impugned the honour of the Republic. He spoke to me about it several times afterwards and his eye flashed at the recollection of the offence. But in spite of that his gentle nature feared that he had been too severe, and that he ought to have attributed the hostile sentiment expressed to thoughtlessness and immaturity.

It was a grief to him that the country should be plunged into war with Spain, but when once the government had taken action he would allow no impeachment of the motives which actuated the nation. "Though in war," he wrote at that time under the head of "Reflections," "from the unchristian attitude of nations and the lack of thorough Christian education, yet there must be the Christian spirit in the struggle, and the advance to the ideal state when there will be no war. We Christians must have the proper thoughts about Spain, and our conversation must be without bitterness. The avowed principle of humanity must be prominent, and secondary and political motives must

be kept out of the struggle and crushed."
Then he proceeded to speak about the need
of prayer that God would overrule all, and
that petitions should be for those with whom
we were struggling as well as for ourselves.

He was enthusiastically patriotic and it
has been his habit for years to go, when it
was possible, to hear the Fourth of July ora-
tion delivered and the Declaration of Inde-
pendence read. I have been with him on such
occasions and have noted that he listened
with devout attention, as though hearing
some new and sacred thing. The national holiday was filled with religious import to him.
During his illness great care was exercised
lest he should learn of the President's assas-
sination; we felt that if it should come to his
ears the shock might prove fatal. And he
died ignorant of the national calamity.

These are incidents that declare how true
a son of the Republic he was. Matters of ci-
vic as well as those of national interest com-
manded his attention and activity — education, the betterment of the conditions of the
poor, the suppression of vice. He was alive
to the problems of his own immediate neigh-

In Whom was no Guile

bourhood, and his plans were always formed
with reference to their solution. It is about a
year since he entered heartily into the Actors'
Church Alliance, of which he became the
President in this city. I have never seen him
more enthusiastic over any enterprise than
he was in this movement. The world and
every department of life were, according to
his way of thinking,—and it is the proper
way,—God's rightful heritage, and it was a
joy to him to feel that the stage, which has
been so slighted and neglected by religion in
the past, should be willing to come under
the sheltering guidance of the Church. The
last entry but one in his diary has to do with
the Alliance.

It may be asked why a man with such cath-
olic sympathies should have been so little in
evidence publicly. The answer is, because he
was living the hidden life. He was an Israelite in deed, not in name and fame. He had
an actual abhorrence of personal prominence.
Filled as he was with self-depreciation that
led him once and again almost to entreat one
of his associates in work to succeed to his position and allow him to assume a subsidiary

In Whom was no Guile

post, it was impossible for him to be much seen on the surface of life. He was one of the master workers who put their labour in where it tells, down among the foundations. He had a "horror of all loud and brawling life," a "deep love for quiet work among the poor," and a "passion for all that was peaceful and restrained." Indeed it was only a mastering sense of duty that held him of late in his place in city work: his inclinations and a fear of incompetency made him yearn for the repose of the country.

How true a son of the faith he was you know as well as I. He was a Christian indeed. Of course narrow men misunderstood his position. His conception of dogma was of a shore from which you launched out upon the great sea of truth, not of four walls which imprisoned you. He was sympathetic with the various phases of truth for which the different schools of thought in our communion stand. And a perusal of his letters written many years back shows that he anticipated that position of comprehension which is now occupying the thought of the foremost men in the Church. He disclaimed any partisan

In Whom was no Guile

allegiance long since and was content to be
known as a Churchman. But there was no
vagueness or uncertainty in his theological
thought: he was very far from being one of
those nerveless, amiable persons who toler-
ate anything. He held in like contempt those
who by suave sophistries explained away the
creed, and those who by tricks of conscience
quite unintelligible to his honest nature read
into Scripture or the formularies of the
Church, mediæval or self-willed philosophy.

It was his desire to be simply one of the
brotherhood of the ministry, and his dislike
of any differentiation between himself and
other clergy led him to discard as far as possible the title of "father" which attached to
him from his early affiliations. But so pecu-
liarly descriptive of his character was it that
people used it instinctively and it adhered
to him to the last. He was a true Father in
God and his personality graced the name.
The title was of spiritual rather than of ec-
clesiastical significance in his case.

No one who knew him could question his
guilelessness. As in the case of Nathanael,
it was his foremost characteristic. He was

In Whom was no Guile

"frank, simple, with no selfish aims to hide, no doubts to suppress." His soul looked out of his eyes, which were as windows to his inner life. The semblance of a lie he scorned and despised. Had it been possible for him to deceive with his lips, his face would have told the truth. He used to say jokingly that he had a "tell-tale face." And so it was: a face that told of inner beauty and power. Because of his absolute transparency he had no faults which a mere acquaintance could not discern; no effort was made on his part to conceal his defects—"what his all but utter whiteness held for sin." He was just what he seemed to be. Most of us at least have a vein of deceit running through us; we intuitively plot to gain the good opinion of our fellows and cover up our ignorances by assuming the air of knowledge: he on the contrary freely, though unconsciously, made public confession of his faults, and he admitted his ignorance when he did not know a thing, making the occasion an opportunity to gain knowledge. But he had a wisdom that was not learned from flesh and blood, but which is God's special gift to the pure in heart. So accurately did his judgement work, so deep and clear was his insight, that it was safer to be guided by his intuitions than by most men's reasoning.

Enthusiasm usually flags with the cessation of youth, but his perennial interest in all that pertained to life expressed itself in child-like delight. New scenery, new experiences, new friendships, called out bursts of sunlight which set his face aglow with joy. And as to new thought, he was always ready to respond to the invitation, "Come and see." He accepted or rejected nothing without experimental knowledge of its value. Proving all things he held fast to that which was good. His unselfishness was of that interior quality that belongs only to a chastened and developed character. When some triumph or success came to his companions in work it roused in him a delight that was not surpassed when a blessing all his own befell him.

His ambition was to serve, and where he seemed to fall short in his work for others —if, for instance, he imagined that he had failed to reach the people in his preaching—

In Whom was no Guile

it was a great sorrow to him. Not that he
dwelt upon failure in the light of a humili-
ation to himself, but as a lost or squandered
opportunity. Failure was something he ex-
pected as a part of the Christian discipline.
"The men," he wrote in his diary, "who
have abandoned themselves to the ideal service of God, who have sacrificed everything
for the truth, have not from the world's
standpoint been a success. Sooner or later
they have failed. This is true of Christ, His
followers and others." The failure that he
dreaded was that which might be traced to
some neglect or flaw in himself. So after a
sermon or meditation when he felt he had
not held attention, are such entries in his
diary as these: "Need of much more loss
of self in public speaking,—grant it to me,
I pray Thee, O Lord." My purpose "is not
to be as great as another, but to give forth
myself—except I speak as God has spoken
to me and *through* me I am not of much
account, nor am I doing any real spiritual
work." And again, "I was not satisfied with
the preparation of my subject. Theological
and explanatory, but not enough life." Still

In Whom was no Guile

again, "Evening congregation not much in-
fluenced apparently by my course of sermons, but I allow a depression in consequence, which is not right. I should prepare:

> more thoroughly;
> remotely especially;
> in the sight of God;
> in self-forgetfulness;

then go forth from Him with a message from
above."

Little did he realize with his refined mo-
desty that his whole life was a sermon. How
could it be otherwise when he began each
year and each day with some such aspira-
tion and resolution as this: "Be the bearer
of the Divine life in the world, in society,
in business, in the home, in recreation as
well as in the Church. In the Actors' Church
Alliance and the life connected with it, have
in view the bearing witness to God as His
child." Could the Alliance ask for a better
motto for their organization? What was a
commonplace of the spiritual life to him
would be for many of us a counsel of perfection. He once said to me in the course of
a conversation, with that simplicity and un-

consciousness of anything unusual that were
characteristic of him, "Of course I have
long since banished from my life anything
that I would be ashamed to have people
know about. Where one fails is in achieving
the positive righteousness of Christ"—or
words to that effect.

His influence consisted just in this—he
was childlike and guileless. His inner reality shone forth from the depths of a sin-
gularly simple, transparent character. Some
men control multitudes by their intellect,
their forceful will, their masterfulness; but
he by the purity of his personality, the sin-
cerity of his purpose, the integrity of his
life.

Of course the secret of his life, of his insight, his good judgement, his pure patriotism, his loyalty to Christ and the Church,
his blamelessness, was that devotional and
meditative habit which was formed in early
life and maintained to the end. Like Nathanael he was frequently beneath the fig-
tree gazing into the depths of eternal truth,
then applying what he learned to the experiences and tasks of every-day life. "The

In Whom was no Guile

daily gift of himself to God and the resig-
nation as a child to the Father's guidance"—
again I quote his words—lay at the foun-
dation of all else. "The fundamental spiritual life is to commune with God in private
and public," he wrote in his diary a few
months ago. This to him was the meaning
of dedication; no matter what the environ-
ment or occupation of a man, this complete
dedication was possible for and obligatory
upon all, the labourer and the priest, the woman in society and the sister of mercy, without difference or distinction. What God calls
for is "the entire gift without reference to
preconceived form: 'it is a certain character,
not certain acts'" that make up the reality
of dedication.

In thus making quotations from his diary
I am but repeating what you have often
heard him say from this place. But there is
this distinction, what he wrote in his diary
was for his own personal guidance and edi-
fication; when he preached he was giving
forth what he had prepared for the instruc-
tion of others. It is not always, however,
that there is such complete correspondence

[102]

In Whom was no Guile

between the rules which the preacher lays
down for the conduct of his own life and
those which he gives out to his people. He
was like Chaucer's "Poure Persoun of a
Toun:"—

> *This noble ensample to his sheepe he yaf*
> *That firste he wroghte and afterward he taughte.*
>
> .   .   .   .
>
> *But Christés loore, and His Apostles twelve,*.
> *He taughte, but first he folwed it hymselve.*

He was the true pastor; he went before
his sheep. He lived as he asked others to
live—with God in all his thoughts. And he
went from his knees to his work. Thus we
find him recording how he would go to some
difficult undertaking, a perplexing visit perhaps, after "a spiritual morning;" or refer-
ring to how "many useful thoughts about
his work" had come to him in an hour spent
with God; or saying that he must "come
from within to the people as prophet and
priest."

And so the very lovely life moved on,
through storm and sunshine, o'er moor and
fen, o'er crag and torrent, till the night was
gone; always the serene countenance tell-

ing of the peace within even though tempest and earthquake were without. His mother's death was a break in his life from which his sensitive and affectionate nature never recovered. The record of the last days of his loved one and of the hours before the burial which he spent by the body, making the room where she lay "his oratory," as he termed it, is a sacred volume and a lesson in filial love. Since then he has thought much of Paradise and of the time when his body, "with feet toward the dawn," would rest by her side in yonder peaceful cemetery.

The time for his going came upon us unexpectedly, though he was ready. A few weeks since, he went away for a short holiday, during which the last illness seized him. God saw that he had done his work and had need of a fuller rest than the brief respite from labour here which he had planned. While a week ago to-day, almost at this hour, the Church on earth was peering with dim but earnest eyes into the world of invisible things and singing songs about the heavenly intelligences, God bade His angels go to his servant and carry him who was an

In Whom was no Guile

Israelite indeed, without guile, into the bosom of Abraham.

Had it been practicable, we should have
brought his body from Toronto, where he
died, to rest for a brief space before this altar at which he served so well. But it could
not be done, and it was taken directly to his
Pennsylvania home. After a Eucharist in the
village church and the stately Burial Office,
we gathered at his grave and left all that is
mortal

> To rest beneath the clover sod
> That takes the sunshine and the rains,

with the perfume of sweet and chaste flowers, emblematic of his character, pressing the
earthy coverlet of his bed.

> And love will last as pure and whole
> As when he loved us here in Time,
> And at the spiritual prime
> Rewaken with the dawning soul.

God has given His beloved sleep; and we
trustfully leave him in his well-earned rest.

As for ourselves, the day of toil has not
yet closed. Some of us are hastening with
rapid feet toward the western hills. Other

In Whom was no Guile

some are in the noontide heat, bearing the burden of the strong and singing the song of the workers. Nor shall we be less vigorous nor less songful because our comrade has left us. With renewed energy shall we stoop to our problems, seeking to know and do God's will. If for a bit the mists hang low and shut out the light we can at least trust and wait; for God is on our side, the God of Israel who neither slumbers nor sleeps, the God to whom darkness and light are both alike, the God who is where He was and what He was always, whether the sun shine or the storm-clouds lower. Life here and now is for us to live for all it is worth; and we can do it creditably if we will but commit ourselves to the keeping of Christ and His Church.

To your tasks then, Comrades! Up and be doing, with a smile on your lips and your tools in your hands! For the Lord God Omnipotent reigneth and we are "the people of His pasture and the sheep of His hand."

Be thou faithful unto death, and
I will give thee a crown of life.

The Closing of Stewardship [1]

It is required in stewards, that a man be found faithful. I COR. iv, 2.

RESPONSIBILITY creates manhood. No character can progress without it. It controls the forces of virility and is the father of all nobility and moral greatness. The wise man courts it; the fool shirks it.

Responsibility keeps pace with spiritual development. The more a man carries, the more he is capable of carrying. In later life, if he has been faithful to his trust, he does intuitively and without a conscious output of strength what in earlier days called for deliberate and exhausting effort. God fits the back to the burden and the burden to the back.

On the other hand he who runs from opportunity and quails before responsibility begins forthwith to die interiorly. Degeneration sets in; all the finest human qualities fall into decay; capacity wanes and the end is eternal death.

Mere occupation is of small avail as a

---

[1] *Preached at S. Stephen's Church, Boston, on the Third Sunday in Advent,* 1901.

The Closing of Stewardship

creative force. To occupation must be added
moral purpose before activity is worthy of
true manhood, and of course the essence of
moral purpose is unselfishness. It is a mel-
ancholy fact of science that many a man and
woman are in a state of physical and nervous
wreck because they are persistently denying
their stewardship. They live for themselves;
their activities are empty of worthy purpose;
they open their hands to receive ten times
for every once they extend them to give. The
penalty of such an existence is as unerring
as it is appalling—it issues in the atrophy
of that divine quality which is humanity's
chiefest treasure and crown. The medicine
that hosts of our army of neurasthenics need
is responsibility gladly accepted. At first it
will be intolerable as the forces of degeneration raise a cry of rebellion at being disturbed and arrested; but eventually life will
triumph over death.

It is plainly apparent to any thoughtful
person, then, that the necessity of recogniz-
ing stewardship is written indelibly in the
constitution of human nature. Before everything else man is a responsible being; that is

to say, he has something in him which is always being interrogated, beckoned, bidden,
and which is capable of answering, moving
out and up, obeying. Stewardship denotes
a relationship between persons, where one
trusts and another responds; where one of-
fers a responsibility and another receives it.
So wonderful a gift is stewardship, so joyous
in its prospect, so satisfying in its substance,
that it is strange that any one refuses to accept it. I suppose, however, that it is due to
the fact that we shut our eyes to the bracing
and stimulating elements in difficulty and
think only of its pains; that we

> .... *love bondage more than liberty;—*
> *Bondage with ease than strenuous liberty.*

But to have drunk deep at the fountain of responsibility is to have tasted of the serenest,
purest joy that life affords.

Man began to be man when God appointed him a steward—for that is the bright side
of the otherwise sad story of the Garden and
its fruit. Human development marched onward as responsibility was enlarged and accepted. The Jewish race was made a steward

The Closing of Stewardship

of monotheistic thought and that glowing
ideal of righteousness which is its constant
companion. Individuals were called to a special guardianship; the prophets had intima-
cies with God not vouchsafed to the common run of mankind. They were stewards
of the inner mysteries and dispensed them
among the race.

I say not God Himself can make men's best
Without best men to help Him.

The greatest act of trust that God performed
was in committing His Chief Steward to
the stewardship of the Jewish people. Our
Lord was trusted to men. "He came unto
his own, and his own received him not." But
in His rejection He found His own opportunity of stewardship. He declared by the
object lesson of His life that the worst becomes the best in the hands of the faithful
administrator. He came not "to do His own
will, but the will of the Father who sent
Him." His motto was *non ministrari sed mi-*
nistrare — not to be ministered unto but to
minister. And so faithful was He to His trust
that when He was stripped of what men call

opportunity, He turned His poverty into wealth and administered it as God's steward —rejection, pain and death rose in an ascending scale of splendour under His touch until they became the treasure-house of the race, and His followers learned to exclaim with simple-hearted ecstasy, "I take pleasure in infirmities, in reproaches, in necessities, in persecutions, in distresses, for Christ's sake." He taught all men of all time that no matter how slight a man's capacity, no matter how wanting in opportunity, each one was a steward of something,—of one pound if not of ten,—and to each He said: "Occupy till I come."

And so to-day you and I stand before God as His stewards. To Him shall we have to present our record when He bids us give an account of our stewardship, "When each man shall have his praise from God." Stewards we are, whether we admit the fact or not; and "it is required in stewards, that a man be found faithful." God expects us to use what we have to the utmost for Him: none can be judged by the standard of another, but each by the opportunity and capacity with which he is

The Closing of Stewardship

endowed. "The ancients pictured opportunity in the figure of a man covered with a forelock on the front of his head and bald behind. Grasp the forelock, seize the opportunity: if not, it passed by you, and you had nothing to lay hold of. Opportunity is bald behind! Yes, time that fleets and opportunity that passes never to return—these are the gifts and the stewardship of every one who hears me."

And we have come to a moment in a stewardship which we have jointly occupied, when the Master says to me, "Give an account of thy stewardship, for thou mayest be no longer steward." A decade of my ministry closes on this Sunday, and with it my relation to you as pastor and companion. A serious man at such a moment finds that there is no need of his *forcing* himself to review the past. The years—yes, the weeks and days—troop by and compel him to take note of them as they rise from the dead in judgement. It is not an easy moment: it is a forecast of the time when the completed career will be rehearsed before the great Judge and Master of all and final rewards and penalties meted out. It is not success or failure that holds the attention at such a time. A man may have had what the observer holds to be a successful career and yet be stung to the quick by the lash of judgement; or he may have been a faithful failure and go through the ordeal with the sweet peace of a commending conscience. Our ideals as God has revealed them to us and given us capacity to realize them are our judge. A man may have been gifted with a rarely vivid conception of duty, and though he has responded to it so as to be lifted head and shoulders above his fellows, yet relatively to them he may have been a faithless steward. We have a loyal and long-suffering friend in the conscience,—may God teach us to obey it at all costs!—and when it ascends the throne of judgement happy are we if we give heed. If it stings and chides it does so for a purpose,—that we may obey its dictates in days to come with greater readiness and joy.

At the close of a stewardship like my own, conscience has a sad work to do. It must speak with its inexorable voice of things done which ought not to have been done, and of things left undone which ought to have been done; of inconsistencies and lapses; of shattered ideals and broken vows; of feeblenesses and faithlessness. But a man moves out to meet such judgement while he quivers under it. Though he says to the Master, "I have been an unprofitable servant; the days of my stewardship have been but poorly fulfilled," he is glad that he has not been spared, that conscience has not been less poignant; glad that the praise of men has not hidden from his eyes the true state of the case; glad that he has been measured by a great rather than a petty standard. He who courts judgement courts life and character, freedom and peace. And what makes the pain of it all bearable and prevents one from being overwhelmed by the knowledge of failure is the thought of God's love and considerateness. To-day as my ten years of stewardship sit in judgement upon me I am constrained to exclaim with an aged servant of Christ at the end of his career and with much more reason—"I am thankful that our God is a merciful God." Perhaps the hardest thing to reckon with is the consciousness of human lives having been in-

jured by neglect of pastoral duty, or slug-
gishness in the performance of it. What can
possibly remedy this? It has gone past recall.
The only conceivable comfort is in the hope
that when we, the injurer and the injured, the
neglecter and the neglected, meet in the home
of perpetual and joyous service above, our
heavenly Father will permit me to spend
my first and fullest efforts in ministering to
those who were injured or passed by here.
It may be that the desire to do this will rescue one from the awful fate of Dives, who
could not even get to Lazarus or Lazarus
to him, because they were separated by such
a moral gulf as made it impossible for their
lives to touch. For a long time I could not
understand how it could be that we would
be able to gain the forgiveness of men whom
we had injured by sins of commission or
omission—God's forgiveness was another
thing and intelligible—until it dawned upon me that we should all be in the same
plight, that no man is without sin against his
neighbour, that in the day of Christ's ap-
pearing every one will be dominated by His
Spirit, and that the long unbroken stretches

of the life of the world to come will afford
opportunity for undoing the ravages of our
badness and unfaithfulness.

Let us review rapidly the character and
terms of the stewardship which you and I
have shared in common. We came to S. Stephen's Church under the guiding hand of
God's Spirit, not for what might be gained,
but for what might be given. The charter
of this Church makes it a trust to be used
in behalf of the people of the neighbourhood in which it stands. It was purchased at
the instance of Bishop Brooks for this spe-
cific purpose: so that all who came here
from elsewhere moved into the arms of a
common responsibility. The parish ceases
to have any reason for its existence if this
is forgotten or neglected. The first duty that
came to hand was to visit thoroughly the
immediate neighbourhood, to put ourselves
in touch with existing agencies for the enrichment of people's lives, and to study the
peculiar conditions in which our lot was cast.
It resulted in the organization of our guilds
and societies, in the establishment of the
mission for such as could not be reached by

the ordinary machinery of parochial life, and the evolution of our industrial and social work. The Rescue Mission from the first has been conducted on the familiar lines of evangelistic work with such modifications as experience suggested, and has been steadily blessed. To some the industrial and social venture—our "neighbourhood work," as it is termed—has not appealed as being spiritual; and I wish, as I turn to it in my thoughts with not a little pride, to emphasize its spiritual quality and its importance to the Church. It is a vicious process of reasoning that differentiates secular and religious, making the former of no account in God's sight. Anything is religious which is done in the name and spirit of Jesus Christ. Nor is this a theory: it is in accord with our Lord's explicit statement. Probably the giving a cup of cold water is the most insignificant and the least costly of any conceivable service. Yet if it be done in the name of a disciple it is commended by our Lord as something that is taken cognizance of in heaven. It is further explicitly stated that to perform works of corporal mercy is to min-

ister to Christ Himself. Such deeds done
from the right motive are lifted up to the
level of worship and adoration. Indeed an
unbiassed student of our Lord's activities
and teaching must conclude that the only
difference between secular and religious is
the result of the inner spirit of the agent.
Anything done from divine motives is essentially spiritual. What makes the body of
a man different from the mere animal or
from inanimate nature is the soul that en-
ergizes it: the difference between the Church
and the world is found in the Spirit resident
within the former, whereas the world in its
evil sense is "society organized apart from"
or independently of that Spirit. In precisely
the same way the motive is the deed in
the individual. The cup of cold water will
doubtless be given to the little ones even if
the Church has no hand in it. But there is a
double loss, a loss to the Church and a loss
to the children, when this is so. A loss to
the Church in that she fails to recognize the
breadth of her responsibility, the dignity of
her stewardship, the penetrative power of
her influence. The Church then becomes a

close corporation—a mere worship insti-
tute instead of the soul of society and the
inspirer of activity. She gets out of touch
with men and her voice grows dull and un-
interesting in their ears. A loss to the children in that they are robbed of the richness
of the deliberate and conscious motive. It is
for this reason that I trust S. Stephen's will
always have in close relation to the parochial life some such enterprise as is now being undertaken in the name of Christ for
His little children. It is the most we can do
for many in whose behalf we would fain do
more. But it is a stewardship that was once
yours and mine; now it is yours. And it is
worth while.

What shall I say of our routine parochial
life? Even there the failures on the part of
your pastor come to rob the joyous mem-
ories that throng the mind of some of their
fragrance. Your unbroken considerateness
that was always ready to excuse defective
service, your generosity and thoughtfulness,
your earnestness and zeal, your simple trust
and confidence, your devoutness and loyalty, bathe me in their sweetness. But side

The Closing of Stewardship

by side with these thoughts rise the search-
ing questions — Have I allowed the excuses
of friends for work undone to quiet the condemning voice of conscience? Have I wasted
my Master's goods through carelessness or
apathy? Have I made your generosity a
starting-point for more vigorous service?
Have I allowed my interior life to grow lack-
lustre and shallow? Has activity outrun devotion? Have I imposed upon your trust?
Have I been scrupulously true to my vows
as priest and pastor? Have sympathy and
patience always found place in my life? To
these and a hundred other queries there is
but one answer, and the answer takes the
form of a cry that has not a little agony in it,
a cry that goes up to the infinite Pity from
the depths of the infinite need: LORD, HAVE
MERCY. It is different now from what it has
ever been before. At the end of a year or on
the occasion of some spiritual awakening,
one was able to make the atonement of repa-
ration — at least to resolve to be truer and
better and more stable — because the old relation remained undisturbed. But now things
are passing from my hands: the old order

The Closing of Stewardship

is finished; my stewardship is complete, and God is asking me if I have been found faithful. And my only reply is, LORD, HAVE MERCY.

But it is not a cry of hopelessness, but of assurance and trust—this appeal for mercy. Whether it is in my case or in yours the mercy comes—comes as it came to S. Peter in the form of a new commission, a new stewardship: "Feed my sheep; feed my lambs." With the closing of the old stewardship a new one opens its portals. Great stretches of opportunity lie ahead with advancing forelock ready to meet the extended hand. You know that I could not separate myself from you lightly, that once and again I have chosen to abide in my place rather than set my hands to new tasks amid new faces. But a day dawned a while ago when unexpectedly and unbidden a voice came and bade me close up the affairs of my stewardship. There was no room for rebellious thoughts: little by little the compulsion of God, so tender, so patient, so inflexible, bent me away from all I love until my face was immovably fixed toward the setting sun,

The Closing of Stewardship

where my last and hardest responsibility
has its home — and its home is mine. I am
glad it is to a difficult task I go; that no
soft places invite my feet away from you,
my friends.

To-day two[1] of us snap the pastoral tie
that has bound us to you. No
more as your official lead-
ers shall we speak to you —
though you will always be
ours and, as I trust, we yours. Those to
whom I have given just cause for offence
or grief will, I am sure, forgive me. Those to
whom I have been of any service will, I believe, strive to live worthily of their high
calling in Christ Jesus our Lord. "And the
very God of peace sanctify you wholly: and
I pray God your whole spirit and soul and
body be preserved blameless unto the coming of our Lord Jesus Christ," when "each
man shall have his praise from God." In the
meantime it behooves us to bind upon our
brow the inscription: "It is required in stewards, that a man be found faithful."

[1] *Rev. H. R. Tal-
bot was also under
appointment by the
Board as a mission-
ary in Manila.*

THE END

www.ingramcontent.com/pod-product-compliance
Lightning Source LLC
Chambersburg PA
CBHW071819090426
42737CB00012B/2140